The Light Will Shine

A STUDY FOR ADVENT

Resource Book

CAROL J. MILLER

D1517764

the KERYGMA
program

Art and Layout: Kathy Boykowycz

© The Kerygma Program, 1999. All rights reserved. Except where noted in the manuscript, portions of this publication may not be reproduced, stored in an electronic system, or transmitted in any form or by any means, electronic, mechanical, photocopy, recording or otherwise, without the prior written permission of the copyright owner. Brief quotations may be used in literary reviews.

The Light Will Shine is published and distributed by The Kerygma Program, Suite 205, 300 Mt. Lebanon Boulevard, Pittsburgh, PA 15234.
Phone: 800/537-9462, FAX: 412/344-1823

ISBN 1-882236-44-0

The Kerygma Program
300 Mt. Lebanon Blvd.
Pittsburgh, PA 15234

CONTENTS

Introducing Rev. Dr. Carol Jean Miller

Dr. Miller is an ordained elder in the United Methodist Church. The recipient of several academic honors, she earned the B.A. degree from Illinois Wesleyan University and M.Th. and D.Min. degrees from Perkins School of Theology, Southern Methodist University. For the last twenty-eight years she has been in pastoral ministry, serving churches in Arkansas, Texas, Pennsylvania and Wisconsin. She is currently Pastor of Oak Creek Community United Methodist Church in Oak Creek, Wisconsin.

Dr. Miller and her husband have two grown daughters, Heather and Mary.

During the last seventeen years, Dr. Miller has written numerous articles and curriculum materials for the United Methodist Publishing House. Her specialty is adult education, but she has authored publications for all age groups from elementary students to senior high school youth. She has written both the *Resource Book* and the *Leader's Guide* for **Good News for All: The Gospel of Luke**, as well as the *Resource Book* for **Into the World: The Acts of the Apostles**.

Foreword

On a purely liturgical level, Advent is a four-week period, beginning with the Sunday in November nearest to the 30th, in which the church, rejoicing in Christ's first coming, looks forward to Christ's coming again. On a more practical level, it is one of the busiest seasons of the year in both its religious and secular aspects. Unfortunately, this activity, however well-intentioned it may be, often obscures the deep significance of the season. "Santa" and "Savior" often create wildly contrasting and conflicting images and meanings for this season which has such a rich history and holds such a significant place in the church year.

This study is designed to provide fresh perspectives on the journey through Advent to Christmas and beyond, and to highlight the underlying message of the traditional scripture texts and themes for the season. But more than that, this study will also make the meaning and message of those texts come alive for you today. It is hoped that you will be equipped to see beyond the "hustle and bustle, glitter and glamour" of "commercial Christmas" to the "good news of great joy" that forms the very foundation of our faith.

In order to gain the most from this study, participants need to make a serious commitment to the group sessions. Read each chapter prior to the group meetings. Stop to look up the **Basic Bible References** (in bold) as you read. Look up the references which are prefaced by the word "Read"; they are important also. And while you are involved in this study, look at your own attitudes toward and observances of the Advent and Christmas seasons, as well as those of your congregation as a whole. What is God calling you to do through this study? In what new directions should you be headed? And, at the end of the study, think seriously about how your understanding of Advent and Christmas has changed. What new understandings have you reached? Where will you go from here?

Preparing for the Group Sessions

It will be helpful for you to approach the work you are about to undertake in a systematic way. We suggest the following process:

1. Obtain a good study Bible with notes and cross references for each section of the text. This will be the major resource for your study. Several are available, including the *New Oxford Annotated Bible with Apocrypha (NRSV), The Oxford Study Bible with Apocrypha,* and the *New Jerusalem Bible.* The *New Revised Standard Version* is the

translation on which this course is based. Quotations of the biblical texts are from this version, unless otherwise noted. However, you will be able to engage effectively in the study with another translation.

2. Review the format of this *Resource Book*. Note that each chapter begins with a **Summary**. The **Basic Bible References** for the chapter follow. These passages are the primary ones you should read to prepare for the group sessions. They are printed in bold type in the text. Many other references will also be listed in the text. They will help to reinforce, elaborate or explain the subject being considered. A **Word List** containing terms or phrases from the Bible references or this *Resource Book* which may be new to you is also included.

At the end of each chapter you will find several items **For Further Study and Reflection**. The first section recommends texts to be included in your "Memory Bank." These are familiar passages that are so central to knowledge of the Bible that you should be able to recall their content or to recite them. The section suggests "Research" projects which will enrich your grasp of the material, but are not essential. Lastly, there are comments and questions for "Reflection" which will challenge you to explore further the issues raised in the chapter.

3. When you are dealing with a particular part of the *Resource Book*, read the **Basic Bible References** before you begin. Then read them again when they come up in the body of the text. Those references preceded by the word "Read" but not in bold are also very important. You should make every effort to review them. Also be aware of the items in the Word List, making sure that you discover in the text the meaning of any unfamiliar word or phrase.

4. Keep an open mind. Do not let the fact that the stories and sayings in this study are familiar lead you to skip over the discussion. Try to come to the study with an eagerness to hear what the text has to say, even if it may say something quite different than you expected.

5. Be alert to what the Advent and Christmas texts have to say for us today and for the world in which we live. The Scriptures deal with human beings and their relationship to God. These are constants in all times and places.

6. Above all, surround your study with prayer and with a willingness to learn something new. Step into the past with the author of "The Light Will Shine" and with God, and find your future.

1

SUMMARY

The Scriptures for the first Sunday of Advent look forward to the Final Coming (Advent) of Christ and the consummation of history. This fulfillment of history spells disaster for those who have ignored God and God's will. It is, however, deliverance for the community of people who live their lives alert to the daily demands of the will of God. The Old Testament texts chosen by the Church speak both of the fearsome justice of God and of the final fulfillment of all the promises of God. The Gospel texts center on the need to be watchful and alert; not allowing the tasks and events of everyday life to distract us from living our lives in the knowledge of God's supreme power. The epistle texts speak to the way people living the gospel message respond to others with love and compassion.

BASIC BIBLE REFERENCES

Old Testament: Jeremiah 33:14-16
                   Isaiah 64:1-9

Gospel: Matthew 24:36-44
                   Luke 21:25-36

Epistle: Romans 13:11-14
                   1 Corinthians 1:3-9

WORD LIST

Messiah

Final Advent

Apocalyptic

1 Watchful Expectancy

Where Is History Headed?

The Church for most of its life has begun the Advent season by centering on the final fulfillment of God's purposes in human history. Why is Messiah coming? What is he announcing? What does he usher in? Beginning with the call of Abraham (Genesis 12:1), the Scriptures record the acts of God as God seeks to reunite rebellious humanity with himself. The promises of God center in the promise that God's will shall ultimately be done in all its fulness. God will be with God's people and the kingdom of God will be reality (see Revelation 21:3-4). Any persons or situations, including death, which attempt to destroy God's communion with God's people will be destroyed. Messiah's coming is both announcement and guarantee that the promises of God are being fulfilled. Our actions do not bring that fulfillment, which the New Testament calls the kingdom. It is coming because God is bringing it. We are called to get in line with what is already breaking in to human history and will come to fruition at the Final Advent.

Read Jeremiah 33:14-16. This text was probably not originally speaking of the Messiah, but more likely was a promise that during a particular time of unrest the nation of Israel, God's servant people, would not cease to exist. The promise of a ruler descended from the line of David, the greatest of Israel's kings, later became associated with the description of God's Messiah—the One who would lead God's people back to God. The Church sees in this text that this promise of God has been fulfilled in a much grander way than the original writer could have known. The one described as "a righteous Branch" is seen in the coming of Christ.

In **Isaiah 64:1-9** the tone is much different. Here the prophet is begging for a mighty epiphany of God now. This section of Isaiah was probably written after Judah, the southern kingdom, had returned from exile in Babylon. The temple at Jerusalem had been destroyed. Israel's God was mocked as not being strong enough to save his people. It is the mocking of God that puts the prophet in agony: "O that you would tear open the heavens and come down . . .to make your name known to your adversaries." If God would only come down into human history, the world would see God's majesty. Isaiah then pleads with the righteous God not to abandon God's sinful people who have brought all their troubles on themselves (verses 5-6). The themes here are the greatness and righteousness of God, the sin of the people which has destroyed their relationship with God, a cry of repentance, and a plea for mercy—a plea for God to be with God's people. It is God's coming into our history that both judges and saves us. This is a central theme for the first Sunday in Advent: Jesus comes as both Judge and Savior. The plea for God to "tear open the heavens and come down" is echoed in the closing words of the Bible: "Come, Lord Jesus." (Revelation 22:20b).

In Malachi the theme is one of joy and fear. Read Malachi 3:1-4. The people delight in God's covenant of love and security. But have they been living their lives as a response to that covenant with God? When the messenger of the covenant comes, he will come with the power of a refiner's fire to make them presentable before Almighty God. The Old Testament ends on the question, "But who can endure the day of his coming. . . ?" (verse 2). This is a question that will lead directly into the preaching of John the Baptizer in weeks two and three of Advent.

Focus on the Final Advent

None of what has been said so far sounds very "Christmassy." It certainly is not designed to sell merchandise! Why does the Church focus on the Final Advent (sometimes called the Second Coming)? The answer comes as we answer the questions: What are we celebrating at Christmas? What does the coming of Christ mean? If in Jesus we see the promises of God coming to pass: promises to be with God's people; promises of the fulfillment of all that life can be; promises of justice and life, then it is the sure hope of the final consummation of history, the fulfilling of God's will, that we celebrate at Christmas. We are not ready to celebrate Christmas until we understand that the God who comes is the God of both justice and mercy. Without looking to where God is leading us, the celebration of God's coming is meaningless. In the words of theologian Fred Gealy:

> By omitting observance of the Final Advent we trivialize the first. A valid observance would confront us with the God who comes both to judge and to redeem. Only when the Final Advent forms the backdrop for the First do both Advents get their full Christian meaning.[1]

Watch and Wait

Thomas Jefferson once said, "I tremble for my country when I consider that God is just." That is at least part of the message of the gospel readings for the first Sunday of Advent. The fact that God is just sets the unjust trembling. If God is bringing to fulfillment God's will in human history, then there will be no place for injustice. The God of mercy would not be merciful if he allowed others to continue to be victimized for eternity. C. S. Lewis speaks of the final destruction of injustice:

> Either the day must come when joy prevails and all the makers of misery are no longer able to infect it; or else forever and ever the makers of misery can destroy in others the happiness they reject for themselves.[2]

Read Matthew 24:36-44 and Mark 13:32-37. The emphasis in these passages is on being ready to participate in the fulfillment of history; the fulness of what the gospels call the kingdom of God. The message is clear: the priorities of our lives must center around the will of God—justice, love, mercy, forgiveness, life, wholeness, reconciliation, joy. If we are conscious of God's presence in the little "advents" of every day, we will already be in line with what is yet to come. The Christian life is lived with the will of God as its goal. The things the Christian does are done deliberately, trusting that the final consummation of life is abundant life lived solely on God's terms. We live our lives on alert. Until we are consciously aiming our lives toward the promises of God we are not ready to celebrate Christmas.

---

1   Fred D. Gealy, *Celebration*, 1969, Graded Press, The Methodist Publishing House, page 16.

2   C. S. Lewis, *The Great Divorce,* Simon and Schuster, New York, New York, 1974, page 118.

Read Luke 21:25-36. The imagery here is more apocalyptic, but the core message is the same. Be on the watch! Do not let the mundane tasks of day-to-day life become the be-all and end-all of life. If they are, we will miss the real goals of life and end up out of sync with the purposes of God. The Christian must cultivate ways of staying alert and centered on what is important. Active life in the Christian community, prayer, meditation and study, and putting into practice compassion, forgiveness and mercy are some of the ways the Christian avoids being lulled to sleep by the routine of every day.

The Behavior of Love

Focusing on the future profoundly impacts the present. **Read Romans 13:11-14.** Paul's call to "wake from sleep" is the same as Jesus' call to "watch." Advent is our wake-up call to look again at how we are living our lives and to what ends. Deeds done "in the light" are deeds of which we have no need to be ashamed. Those deeds all center in right actions toward the neighbor. **Read 1 Corinthians 1:3-9** and 1 Thessalonians 3:9-13. Paul enumerates the "fruits of the Spirit" in Galatians 5:22-23. All of them have to do with loving actions and attitudes toward other people. These fruits are gifts, not qualities earned by force of character. Those who are open to God's future receive God's gifts that enable them to live in the present and in the future. In 1 Thessalonians, Paul especially mentions the young church's love for "one another," a technical term in the New Testament that always means fellow Christians. The gifts of love and mercy are first given in the Christian fellowship and from there are shared with others.

On Not Rushing the Season

The season of Advent which prepares us for Christmas focuses our minds, wills, and hearts not on the "end of the world" but on the beginning of life as God would have it lived—the kingdom in all its fullness, "abundant life." That life is possible when God has purged us of all that is not in line with life as God would have it lived and when we respond to the future that is already becoming present. Christians live between the First Advent and the Last Advent. We are granted a foretaste of that final life of love and joy as we deliberately and consciously live the life of mercy and love in our relationships with others. Only when we hear and incorporate the message of the Final Advent does the celebration of the First Advent make any sense. Only when we have truly celebrated the Advent season are we ready for Christmas.

For Further Study and Reflection

Memory Bank

1. Memorize Malachi 3:1-4

2. Memorize the fruits of the Spirit in Galatians 5:22-23.

Research

1. In a Bible dictionary such as the **Interpreter's Dictionary of the Bible**, read the article on the Exile to Babylon

2. Research the title "Christ" or "Messiah" looking especially at its meaning in the Old Testament and its connection with King David's dynasty.

Reflection

1. Think about this sentence: "If God does not judge us, there is no justice." Reread the C. S. Lewis quote on page 5. How is God's judgment part of God's mercy and love?

2. Have you ever skipped to the last page of a book to see how it turned out? How is the coming of Christ into our history like that? What do we know about the end of history because of Jesus' coming?

3. Why are some people in such a rush for Christmas that they want to ignore Advent? List at least three reasons why the Church should emphasize Advent.

2

SUMMARY

John, as the one who announces Messiah's arrival, and as the one who outlines the necessary preparations for the first Advent, occupies two Sundays in the Church calendar. John proclaims the need both for repentance and the evidence of repentance. Readings from both the Second and Third Sundays in Advent will be looked at in this session.In the midst of the call for repentance in the second and third weeks, the third Sunday in Advent also breaks into songs of joy. John's message is, after all, good news: repentance and life with God are possible! The nature of the Messiah who is coming is implied by the expectations of ethical behavior on the part of those who have repented of their previous way of life. Loving behaviors toward the neighbor and especially those of the Christian community are demanded of those who follow Messiah.

BASIC BIBLE REFERENCES

Old Testament: Isaiah 11:1-10

Isaiah 40:1-11

Isaiah 35:1-10

Isaiah 61:1-4, 8-11

Gospel: Luke 3:1-18

Matthew 3:1-12

John 1:19-34

Matthew 11:2-11

Epistle: 1 Thessalonians 5:16-24

Romans 15:4-13

2 Peter 3:8-15a

James 5:7-10

WORD LIST

Repentance

Escaton

2 John The Baptizer

The Advent of God

Read Isaiah 11:1-10. In Isaiah's words (which originally may have been an idealized description of one of the kings of Israel) the Church saw a description of the Messiah's nature. He is a descendant of David—Jesse was David's father. He is filled with God's own Spirit. His reign is marked by wisdom and by justice for the needy. He is the destruction of those who oppose God. When he reigns, peace will flow through every living creature. All nations will be drawn to Israel's God. This is the promise of God's future which God will bring.

Read Isaiah 40:1-11. In Isaiah's words of comfort to those returning from the Babylonian Exile, the Church and the gospel writers heard the promise of the advent of God on the stage of history. "Here is your God!" God's word is forever. The will of God outlasts all the fading glory of those people who think they rule the earth. God is coming with justice, with forgiveness, and with compassion for the weak and needy. The Advent texts continually challenge their hearers to look to God's future and prepare themselves for it.

What Then Shall We Do?

Read Luke 3:1-18, Matthew 3:1-12, and **Mark 1:1-6.** All three gospel writers identify John the Baptizer with the voice of Isaiah 40:3. Luke introduces John in the same way that the prophets of the Old Testament were introduced: "the word of God came to John" (see the opening verses of Jeremiah, Ezekiel, Hosea, and Isaiah).

The prophet John has two messages and therefore appears on two Sundays in Advent (second and third). His first message is that the promised Messiah, the "anointed one" of God is at hand. The second message is that radical preparations must be made in order to be ready to receive Messiah. The season of Advent begins again the story of our salvation in Christ. John appears in the doorway of the covenant community roaring: "Repent, for the kingdom of heaven is near!" The Lord is breaking into human history to reconcile God's rebellious people to God. Anyone who is receptive to God must renounce the self-centered ways of the past and begin to live a life that is in line with God's ways and will.

What does John mean by the word "repent?" Our English word comes from the French, "repense," "think again." In order to repent we must first stop to look at the way we have been thinking—assumptions about priorities, about what is important in life. We must then look closely at our lives: How have we been living them? Where are we headed? What gives our lives focus? Are our lives directed by God or by our own self-serving ends? What do our lives have to offer God? These questions form the true mood of Advent. It is God who is coming to us, but we must also turn toward God. Repent, then, also has the sense of turning around, turning away from the old priorities and actions to new priorities and new actions which are centered on God's will instead of our own.

John's call to repent assumes that new and ethical actions will replace the old, self-centered ways. Hence his warning in Matthew 3:7-8 when he sees the Pharisees and Sadducees coming: "Bear fruit worthy of repentance." By coming to receive John's baptism the people are indicating that they have repented of their previous sinful way of life. If that is so, their current actions should be able to give plenty of evidence of the change. True repentance results in a changed life with changed priorities.

Getting Specific

In Luke 3:11-14 three different groups of people approach John. He is specific about the kind of fruits that those who have truly repented will perform. First, the crowd is instructed to share. The math is not difficult: If you have two tunics and your neighbor has none, even things out. Likewise with food or any other necessity. In the fourth century A.D. Augustine contended that anyone who had more than he needed possessed the goods of another. Those who have truly repented do not look first or only to themselves. Our attitudes toward material possessions say a great deal about our relationship to our neighbors. Our relationship to our neighbors says a great deal about our relationship with God. The traditions that prevail both inside and outside the Church during the Advent season of gathering clothes, gifts, and food for those in need stem from this text.

The second group to approach John is composed of tax collectors, traitors who collected taxes for the Roman oppressors and extorted more money to line their own pockets. John tells them that getting all you can for yourself by whatever means necessary is not in line with the coming of Messiah. "The bottom line" is not the bottom line for John. Repentance demands that the welfare of the neighbor be the bottom line. We cannot build a loving relationship with God on a foundation of selfish deeds.

The third group is soldiers. They may have been Jews who were recruited by King Herod for his service. Jews were not conscripted into the Roman army. No doubt they would have been tempted to intimidate civilians in order to supplement their wages. They, too, if they are truly turning from their old, selfish ways, must be compassionate and concerned for others instead of doing whatever they can to get ahead.

Advent, then, is a call to show the integrity of our repentance by replacing the self-centered with the God-centered. Being God-centered results in actions which are neighbor-centered. Preparing for Christmas does not mean buying fresh tinsel, but preparing our inmost selves to stand face-to-face with the Incarnation of Almighty God. To ignore Advent makes the Christmas celebration worthless.

Who Is John?

Read Luke 3:15-18. John's preaching apparently strikes a chord in the hearts of his listeners, for they begin to wonder if he himself might be Messiah. John had a large following of disciples, even into the time of the early Church. But the gospel writers take pains to record John's understanding of his role. **Read John 1:19-34**, Matthew 3:11-12 and Mark 1:7-8. John's baptism is a simple baptism with water to indicate the people's sense of repentance. Messiah will put God the Holy Spirit into their minds and hearts and will destroy all that is unholy about them. John is a simple messenger of the truth. Messiah will separate truth from falsehood. Messiah is power. **Read Matthew 11:2-11**. Jesus himself pays homage to John. John's message cannot be ignored, Jesus tells the people, for John is indeed the prophet of the Messiah spoken of in Malachi 3:1.

The Early Church Lives the Message

The epistle texts for the second and third weeks of Advent speak about the demands of love in the Christian community. Christians are to look to the needs of all neighbors regardless of the neighbors' religion. But before that can truly happen, Christians must give and receive that selfless love in the context of the Christian community. Christ formed the Church in order that his followers should especially love and care for one another. The Church is a tiny outpost of the kingdom of God and must reflect the kingdom's values. This caring community would serve as a beacon for the world to see what God's love looks like lived out in human community (see John 13:34-35). If love and concern for fellow Christians in the covenant community is not a priority, how will Christians ever truly love those beyond the community of faith?

Read Romans 15:4-13. The term "one another" in the New Testament always refers to fellow Christians. There is to be the unity and acceptance in the fellowship that Christ's love brings. In Paul's day Christians who were converts from Judaism had a hard time accepting into the fellowship Christians who were former pagans, Gentiles. Paul contends that no one's background or race matters in the Church—only the fact that each is bound to Jesus Christ matters. This is Paul's prayer for the young Church in Philippians 1:3-11.

Read 1 Thessalonians 5:16-24 and Philippians 4:4-13. Here are lists of the kinds of deeds that naturally fill the Christian life. These are not "to do" lists. These are descriptions of what the individual (and the faith community) that is bound to Christ is like. If these deeds and thoughts are not your deeds and thoughts, then your relationship to Christ is called into question. The Advent texts call us to examine the integrity of our life in Christ. **James 5:7-10** and **2 Peter 3:8-15a** caution the Christian not to become impatient, but to be full of good deeds as we wait for the consummation of history.

Joy Breaks Forth

The Old Testament readings for the third Sunday interject a new note into the Advent themes. The preaching of John may be caustic and sound threatening, but it is, after all, good news (Luke 3:18). Joy breaks out in the third Sunday—Gaudete or "Joy" Sunday.

Repentance is possible! God is offering us reconciliation with God. Forgiveness is on the way. **Read Isaiah 35:1-10**. Isaiah looks to that culmination of history (the eschaton) when God's will is fully done. In that final time, life will bloom where life was previously not possible. The weak will be strong, the death-dealing desert will gush forth with water, a powerful image for a desert-dwelling people. The announcement of God's coming among the people gives courage. "Be strong. Do not fear!" But there is also a warning in Isaiah. Those who do not follow God's will, those who choose the ways of evil will not be part of the final reality. They are excluded. But those who follow God will rejoice in God.

Read Isaiah 61:1-4, 8-11. God's messenger comes with good news for all who suffer and are oppressed. There is news of comfort, favor, release, and freedom. The God of justice is at hand to redress all the grievances of those who yearn for God's love. Joy bubbles to the surface in this message of hope. Jesus himself defines the whole purpose of his coming with the words of Isaiah 61:1-2 as he inaugurates his ministry (see Luke 4:16-21).

The same joyful message of salvation and release is found in the concluding song in Zephaniah 3:14-20. Even though the call to repent strikes fear into the human heart, it is at the same time the message that God's salvation is at the gates. We are not a forgotten people doomed to live a meaningless life of pain and disappointment. God Almighty remembers his suffering people. The road to repentance ends at the house of joy!

For Further Study and Reflection

Memory Bank

1. Memorize Isaiah 35:3-7.

2. Memorize Isaiah 61:1-4. This is the portion of Isaiah that Jesus read in the synagogue at Nazareth when he began his ministry.

Research

1. In a Bible dictionary such as the **Interpreter's Dictionary of the Bible** look up the term "repentance" especially as it is used in the New Testament.

2. In a Bible dictionary research John the Baptist, especially his teaching and his baptism.

3. Look up the term "one another" in a concordance. Read several of the passages cited. What is the obligation of the Christian to the Christian community?

Reflection

1. One might think that a dramatic figure such as John the Baptizer would expect dramatic signs of repentance, such as turning from a life of crime. But when asked what they are to do, John tells the penitent to share an extra shirt; to pass along some food to someone in need. How do these little things draw us closer to God? What are the everyday sins that you need to repent in order to be ready for Jesus?

2. In what ways does your local church reflect the kind of selfless love of "one another" that the epistle readings talk about? Is your congregation consciously working to be a fellowship of love that is a model for the community outside your church?

3. How are you preparing yourself to be truly ready for Christmas?

3

SUMMARY

Christmas signals the fulfillment of all God's promises to the covenant people Israel. The texts for the fourth Sunday of Advent tie Jesus to the Old Testament. He is the descendant of David. Jesus is the promised Messiah. But he is also the Son of God. Through a series of dreams and songs the Scripture texts highlight Jesus' nature and mission. The epistle texts speak of Jesus' divine and human natures.

BASIC BIBLE REFERENCES

Old Testament: 2 Samuel 7:1-11, 16
                    Micah 5:2-5a

Gospel: Matthew 1:18-25
                    Luke 1:26-38

Epistle: Romans 1:1-7
                    Hebrews 10:5-10

WORD LIST

Angel
Immanuel
Magnificat

3 The Fulfillment of All Promises

The Announcement

Read Luke 1:26-38. Gabriel appears several times in late Judaism as a messenger of God. The word "angel" is derived from the Greek word for "messenger." Gabriel comes to Mary in the sixth month of Elizabeth's pregnancy. The Annunciation to Mary is more than a beautiful story. It conveys an important theological point. Jesus is to be the Messiah for whom many Jews hoped. It is his reign that will be eternal; all the promises of God will be fulfilled in the kingdom which he will inaugurate. Gabriel also refers to Jesus as "Son of God." This is not part of the Jewish understanding of Messiah. Jesus stands in a relationship to God that has no equal.

The promise to David that one of his descendants would always be on the throne of Israel became in late Judaism part of the description of the Messiah. **Read 2 Samuel 7:1-11, 16**. It is here that God makes the covenant with the house of David. (Matthew refers to Jesus as "son of David" on numerous occasions). We will note that every Gospel ties Jesus firmly to Judaism. He is the fulfillment of all the promises God has made to the covenant people.

The Visitation

On receiving her startling news, Mary hurries to her kinswoman Elizabeth to share the announcement. Read Luke 1:39-55. Note especially that Elizabeth speaks through the power of the Holy Spirit. It is God's own Spirit that causes Elizabeth to bless Mary and Jesus. Elizabeth is also the first person in Scripture to refer to Jesus as "my Lord," and that even before Jesus is born! The way Elizabeth greets the news of Jesus' impending birth is clearly the way all those who love God should react. This is good news. The one who is coming is Lord and we are privileged that he comes to us.

Elizabeth makes yet another important point in her short but powerful speech: Mary is blessed not because of any good works she might have done that would cause God to choose her. Mary is blessed because "she believed" that God would keep his promise to her. It is putting one's trust in God and in the future that God is bringing that constitutes blessedness. Mary is a far cry from King Ahaz, whom we will meet shortly.

A Sign

Read Micah 5:2-5a. As in the Annunciation, this text also ties Jesus to the promise to David, since Bethlehem was David's "home town." Bethlehem is an ancient town five miles from Jerusalem. The name can mean "house of bread." Ephrathah designates the specific region where Bethlehem is located. The ruler mentioned in verse 2 was probably David himself, as the prophet Micah looked back on the beginnings of Israel's glory days. Verse 3 refers to the time when Judah, the southern kingdom, was taken into exile in Babylon. The early Church, as it often did with such passages, took this Scripture and recast it to speak about deeper meanings than it originally had. Bethlehem is indeed to be the place of a great ruler whose kingdom will last forever. But it is no mere political vice-regent, but God himself who comes to reign. The image of the shepherd, which Jesus used in the Gospels to describe himself, strengthens the Church's reason for using this text to describe Jesus.

She Will Bear a Son

By the fourth Sunday in Advent, which can come as late as December 24, Christmas is indeed beginning to shine through the cracks! The text from Matthew, however, is the only one that specifically mentions Jesus' birth. Throughout his Gospel Matthew continually ties the events of Jesus' life to the Hebrew Scriptures. He does so in his Christmas text.

Read Isaiah 7:10-16. This text was written about a time seven hundred years before the birth of Jesus when Judah (the southern kingdom) was under attack. Ahaz, King of Judah, had been promised by God's prophets that Ahaz' enemies would not prevail in their attempt to replace the Davidic monarchy. Ahaz does not trust God's word and is attempting to make foreign political alliances in order to save his throne. God tells Ahaz to choose any sign he likes and God will produce it as a testimony to God's word. Ahaz refuses—with false piety. God chooses a sign. A young woman will bear a son and name him "Immanuel" which means "God with us." Before that child is weaned, the land of the two kings that threaten Ahaz and the throne of David will be "deserted."

The text in Hebrew does not use the Hebrew word for virgin. But when the text was translated into Greek almost three hundred years before the time of Jesus, the Greek translator used the Greek word for virgin. This version was somehow picked up by the early Church which saw in it a reference to the birth of Jesus.

Read Matthew 1:18-25. Matthew focuses his telling of the Christmas story on the supernatural birth of Jesus. At several points in the Old Testament there is a motif of women who become pregnant when reason says it is not possible. Sarah (Genesis 18:1-15), Rebekah (Genesis 25:21), Rachel (Genesis 30:1-2, 22-24), and Hannah (1 Samuel 1:5, 19-20). All these stories remind the reader that the future is a gift from God. Just as the story of God's covenant people began with a barren elderly couple to whom God gave a son, so now the salvation story is completed by the action, not of persons, but of God. Matthew is not asking the reader to believe in Jesus because of a connection to an Old Testament text, or because of an impossible happening. Matthew wants his readers to see that the coming of Jesus is God's will. In the naming of Jesus, God's will for God's people is made clear. In Hebrew "Joshua" (in Greek Jeshua or Jesus) means "God is salvation."

The Magnificat

Read Luke 1:46-55. This is not one of the Gospel readings in the lectionary, but it does find a place where the psalter would usually be. The Latin term for this song is the Magnificat. It is the song of Mary and within it are several important statements about the nature and work of the coming Messiah. Exactly who is it that we are expecting with such excitement? What is going on here?

Mary rejoices in the coming of Jesus as the eternal establishment of all the promises that God has made to the covenant community, Israel. He has helped his servant Israel "in remembrance of his mercy." God's faithfulness has always been reason for rejoicing. But in the birth of Jesus the will of God for God's people is being brought to light in all its power. The proud and the arrogant rulers of the world are scattered and those who put their trust in God are elevated. The self-centered rich receive nothing, but those who were in want are satisfied. Here is a picture of what reality finally looks like. As we heard from John the Baptizer, it is time to get in line with reality. God's promises in Jesus are so sure that Mary can speak of them in the past tense.

The View From the Epistles

Read Romans 1:1-7. Paul opens his letter to Rome with a powerful statement about who Jesus is. First he makes it clear that Jesus is the fulfillment of the Old Testament promises (verse 2). The Holy Scriptures refer to the Hebrew Scriptures, since the New Testament had yet to be written. Paul also makes the connection between Jesus and King David. But Paul is taking the discussion in a different direction. He intends to say two equally important things about Jesus Christ: that Jesus was human, a descendant of David; and that he is Son of God, divine. For Paul, Jesus' position as Son of God has nothing to do with any concept of a virgin birth as it does in Luke 1:35. For Paul, Jesus is Son of God because God has declared him to be so. This declaration of Jesus' sonship came in the symbol of the resurrection.

Read Romans 16:25-27. This is the closing benediction of Paul's letter. He speaks of the revelation of the mystery hidden for long ages past; that is, the knowledge of God that is revealed in the incarnation—God being made known in human flesh. The purpose of Jesus' coming is so all nations might know and obey God through him. This gracious God, who makes himself known to all people through Jesus is worthy of praise and glory.

Finally **read Hebrews 10:5-10**. The author of Hebrews uses the words of Psalm 40:6-8 as the words of Christ to God. The writer makes use of the words of the psalm to make a point that he makes many times in Hebrews; namely that Christ's sacrifice on the cross has made unnecessary all other sacrifices. His understanding of the incarnation is that Christ came into the world to be the complete once-for-all sacrifice for the whole world. Therefore, the Law with its need for sacrifices has been superseded. The words of verse 9 certainly fit the fourth Sunday of Advent as Jesus is about to step onto the stage of history: "See, I have come to do your will, O God!" (NIV).

For Further Study and Reflection

Memory Bank

1. Try memorizing the entire "Magnificat" Luke 1:46-55.

Research

1. In a Bible dictionary such as the **Interpreter's Dictionary of the Bible** research the city of Bethlehem, especially its significance in relation to David and to Jesus.

2. Look up Hannah's song in 1 Samuel 2:1-8 and compare it to Mary's song in Luke 1:46-55.

Reflection

1. Listen to "Behold, a Virgin Shall Conceive" and "O Thou That Tellest Good Tidings to Zion" from Handel's Messiah, and lose yourself in the words and music.

2. Reread the promises of God that Mary recalls in Luke 1:46-55. How are these promises valid for the Church today? Does your congregation show trust in these promises? In what ways?

3. What is it about Jesus that makes him the Christ in your eyes?

4

SUMMARY

The Scriptures for Christmas Eve and Christmas Day focus not so much on the historical occurrence of the birth of Jesus as they do on the theological meaning of Christ's entry into the world. These Scriptures are Christologically centered: they are concerned with who Jesus Christ is in relation to God the Father and in relation to humanity. In addition to describing the nature of Christ, they also focus on the function of Christ as savior and as the self-expression of the nature of almighty God.

BASIC SCRIPTURE REFERENCES

The first Scripture in each section is the text for Christmas Eve. The second is the text for Christmas Day.

Old Testament:	Isaiah 9:2-7
	Isaiah 52:7-10
Gospel:	Luke 2:1-20
	John 1:1-14
Epistle:	Titus 2:11-14
	Hebrews 1:1-12

WORD LIST

Eschatology
"Christ the Lord"
Incarnation

4 The Dawning of Day

The King Reigns

Read Isaiah 9:2-7. Most Christians probably cannot read these words without beginning to hum a few bars from Handel's "Messiah." That is as it should be, for Handel wonderfully set to music some of the most powerful words in all of Scripture. The original subject of Isaiah's words may have been a new king ascending the throne of David, which would make this text a kind of coronation hymn. There are several of these in the Old Testament, principally in Psalms (see Psalm 72 for example). Or it may be a hymn about the ideal king of the eschatological age—that final time when God's will is done completely on the earth. The picture then would be of God's ideal king. The titles listed in verse 6b are the kind that were given to the king as God's anointed servant. "Mighty God" can mean "divine in might" since the king is God's agent.

The word translated "government" by the RSV is a rare word in Hebrew. It can mean "authority" as in the NRSV, "the burden of authority" or the symbol of royal authority, something worn on the royal robes, or perhaps a scepter. This king has the right to rule because it has been laid on him by God.

The Church has always used Isaiah's words to describe Jesus Christ. He is the "great light;" he is the one who lifts up those who are in a land of "deep darkness." It is he who makes joy break out with the defeat of all life's enemies. He is just and righteous and his governing in "justice and . . . righteousness" is forever. He is the long-awaited descendant of David (verse 7). It is no wonder that the church has sent these verses out into the world as a kind of marvelous birth announcement: "Unto us a son is born . . . " (RSV).

Can You See the Herald?

Read Isaiah 52:7-10. These words are written by a different Isaiah than the one who wrote chapter 9. This Isaiah writes to the covenant community that has come home from Exile in Babylon; come home to a shattered nation and a despoiled Jerusalem. Judah had seen itself at war not so much with Babylon as with God. God had punished his people. But with the opening words of Isaiah 40, the war was declared to be at an end: "Comfort, comfort my people, says your God. Speak tenderly to Jerusalem, and say to her that her warfare is ended . . . " (NASB).

In ancient times, the people of a city would wait for a runner to come from the battle to tell the citizens who had won. The watchmen on the towers of the city's walls would strain to see the messenger approaching. When the messenger came within earshot he might well call out the news: "We've won! The battle is over!" Just so in Isaiah 52:7: the news is in and it is good news. Our God reigns! The watchmen on the towers must now tell the whole city the good news, the glad tidings.

Just so is the message of Christmas: our sins have been conquered by our God. The battle is over; God reigns. The waiting of Advent is over; the good news has arrived. Even what has been dead and shattered in our lives is called to come to life and burst into song (verse 9). Christmas is the celebration of God's victory made visible in Jesus. Christmas, then, is to be celebrated with cheers and songs and dancing. Our God reigns!

Peace On Earth!

Read Luke 2:1-20. Here is the most well-known of all the Christmas texts, but it is the text for Christmas Eve, not Christmas Day itself. The Church throughout most of its life has not been as interested in the happenings surrounding Jesus' birth as it has been interested in the theological meaning of those events. Even Luke himself is not primarily interested in the historical event of Jesus' birth. For this scene which at first looks like simple reporting of "facts" is indeed a theological document.

From the beginning of Luke's Gospel there has been a steady stream of individuals telling us who Jesus Christ is, why he has come: Gabriel, Elizabeth, Mary, Zechariah, and now more angels. In Luke's Gospel, angels are often used to bring messages from God. But they are not what is important; the message is important. This message summarizes Luke's Christology.

The message to the shepherds begins with the words "Do not be afraid." God is not coming to terrify the people. As in Isaiah 52 the news is in and it is good news! It will produce joy. In David's city (Bethlehem) the "savior" has been born. The angel identifies him as "Christ the Lord." Both of these designations are unusual. Matthew, Mark and John never use the term "savior." Luke uses it only twice in the Gospel and twice in Acts. It is only used on rare occasions in the Old Testament. It was the pagans who commonly used the term for their gods, for example, "Zeus Savior." The use of the term savior may be to show that the gods of the pagan world cannot compare to Jesus. The combination of titles "Christ the Lord" would not be found in Jewish thinking. The Jewish messiah was not thought of as a divine being. He was to be an agent of God's. The Jews could speak of "the Lord's Christ, " that is, the Lord's anointed, but not of Christ the Lord. The one who has come is Messiah but he is more than Messiah.

The sign of "Christ the Lord's" coming is unusual to say the least: a newborn in a feed trough! The audience to whom this message is addressed is equally odd: shepherds; people of no standing in the community. They are the no-accounts. It is to the nobodys that the angels bring greetings of good news. The heavenly host, the army of God, appears to praise God as well. This history-shattering event that brings glory to heaven brings peace to earth. Heaven and earth share in the joy of this birth. It is difficult to translate the last part of verse 14. It can mean peace to all people or it can mean peace to those with whom God is pleased. The truth is that this message will not bring peace to all; the Herods and Caesars of the world will not be at all pleased with this announcement, for real power is breaking in to knock to pieces the false powers of the dictators and the selfish.

Be aware when reading this text not to substitute belief in angels or babies in mangers for the real message: God has come to deliver us from everything that keeps us separated from God. Whether that news comes via angels or E-mail is not important.

The Christmas Gospel

From early days the Prologue to John's Gospel has been the text for Christmas Day. **Read John 1:1-14**. In these words there is neither angel nor manger, virgin mother nor shepherds. All the stage props have been taken away. What remains is the underlying meaning of what all the stories have been saying. What remains is the unveiling of the divine mystery, the heart of God's love and power "enfleshed" for our salvation.

The opening words "In the beginning" are meant to evoke the identical opening words of Genesis. In that account of creation God speaks (Genesis 1:3) and God's speech becomes visible: "And God said, 'Let there be light!' and there was light." Just so in John's Gospel. The Word is God's self-expression; God's revealing of his nature. Because God is perfect and God's word is true, when God speaks, God's word **is** God. John tells us that God has spoken the self-revealing word; the word that makes God known. And when God spoke "the Word became flesh," "full of grace and truth." Jesus Christ is the "enfleshment," the incarnation, of God.

John says that "He was in the beginning with God. All things came into being through him, and without him not one thing came into being." This is a statement of what is called "the pre-existent logos." The word for "Word" in Greek is logos, from which we get the words "logo" and "logic." The pre-existent logos means that God's self-expression has always been; it is the heart of God. Everything that has ever come into existence has existed because God called it into being. It is not the man Jesus who is pre-existent. It is the nature of God which has been incarnated in Jesus that has existed since before time began.

The motif of light and darkness is prevalent throughout John's Gospel. In verse 9 John refers to the logos as the "true light." Jesus' presence in the world lights up reality. It lights our path. It lights up the dark corners of our minds. Anyone who has stumbled around in a dark room, banging shins on furniture, knows the relief of having someone turn on the light. Then everything is clear; the right path is easy to discern. Jesus is light for this dark world. Not everyone comes to the light. But for those who do, Jesus gives them the power to become "the children of God." The true birth, the important birth has nothing to do with the "will of the flesh." As with the symbol of the virgin birth in Matthew and Luke, it has to do with "the will of God." The incarnation of God's logos is grace, freely given, the undeserved gift of joy.

The Radiance of God

The epistle text for Christmas day is amazingly similar to the text from John's Gospel. **Read Hebrews 1:1-12.** The author of Hebrews (his identity is unknown) begins with God's speaking in earlier days. But now God has spoken "in these last days," "by a Son." Again, the Son is God's self-expression to us. As in John, Hebrews affirms that through the Son, God made the universe. Hebrews spells out in different words precisely the same message that John conveys with his "logos" theology: "The Son is the radiance of God's glory and the exact representation of his being sustaining all things by his powerful word" (NIV). The term "radiance" means the shining rays of the sun. It would be as impossible to separate the Son from the Father as it would be to separate the sun from its shining. The message of John and of Hebrews takes our breath away as we stand in awe of what has happened at Christmas.

In verses 5-12 the author seems to be arguing against a cult of angel worship by showing from Scripture that Christ is superior to angels in every way. Christ is the Son of God. The author of Hebrews would certainly agree that paying attention to the form of the messenger should never be substituted for the message itself. And the message is the love and forgiveness and power of God shining in the face of Christ.

What Then Shall We Do?

Read Titus 2:11-14. This magnificent Christmas message demands a whole-life response from us; an ethical response. Because God's truth has appeared, those who have seen the truth must begin to live by the truth. We live what we really believe. The Christmas announcement calls us to a new way to live this life (verse 12). But the Christmas message is also an announcement of the final consummation of history, the coming of the kingdom in power (verse 13). Just as Advent began with the call to lead life in a new way, so the season closes with the challenge to live this life in the truth of Christ as a preparation for the final coming of God's kingdom.

For Further Study and Reflection

Memory Bank

1. Memorize as much as you can of the prologue to John's Gospel (John 1:1-14). Use it daily as a meditation during the coming Christmas season.

Research

1. Research the beginnings of the celebration of Christmas by the Church. How was the western Church's celebration different from that of the Church in the east (which became Orthodox Christianity)?

2. Do a little research on angels in a good Bible dictionary. Are we in danger in this culture of worshipping angels? Read the Hebrews passage again.

Reflection

1. Write a poem on the theme of light and dark.

2. What does it mean for you to say that God has "conquered" your sins?

5

SUMMARY

The texts for Epiphany Day all celebrate the revealing of God's nature and will for the world. That will or purpose is the communion of God with all people, and the powers of evil (represented by Herod) cannot overcome it.

Epiphany serves as a reminder that the people of God, expressed in the Old Testament as Israel and in the New Testament as the Church, exist solely to celebrate the glory of God and to reflect that glory in the world. When the people of God reflect the light of God into the world around them, all people of every race and tribe can see God—the love, forgiveness, and magnificence of God.

The Epiphany season is, then, in many churches, the season to celebrate world-wide missions; the bringing of the light to all peoples everywhere. The first people from beyond the community of faith to see God reflected in Jesus are represented by the Magi; foreigners to Israel who come to offer worship to Israel's God as revealed in Jesus.

BASIC BIBLE REFERENCES

Isaiah 60:1-6

Matthew 2:1-18

Ephesians 3:1-12

WORD LIST

Epiphany

Magi

Principalities and powers

5 Shine, Jesus, Shine: Epiphany Day

Shine, People, Shine!

Read Isaiah 60:1-6. At first glance the reasons the Church picked this Old Testament Scripture for Epiphany seem obvious: kings coming, camels, gifts of gold and frank-incense all call to mind the Gospel text about the magi. But more is here than that! The word "epiphany" is Greek. It means literally "to show forth," to make manifest. The heart of the message for Epiphany is that God will reveal God's love, power, forgive-ness, and awe-inspiring majesty to all people. The whole world of every race and nation will see the wonder of Israel's God and be drawn in joy to love and serve God. The season following the Christmas season is a time to rejoice that God has called all people everywhere to be in communion with God.

How will the nations, those beyond the chosen people, Israel, behold these glories of God? This is the message of this text from Isaiah. "Arise, shine; for **your** light has come, and the glory of the LORD has risen upon **you**…the LORD will arise upon **you**, and his glory will appear over **you**. Nations shall come to **your** light, and kings to the brightness of **your** dawn."(emphasis mine). The "you" is Jerusalem which is representative of God's people, Israel. It will be through God's people that the world will see God's radiance. The Church sees in this text a call for the people of God to reach out with God's love to people all over the world; not to call them to any one nation, but to call them to become part of the world-wide body of Christ.

This text is set in the days when Judah had returned from Exile in Babylon to find its land and its Temple destroyed. But there is good news: God's tender love and glory will shine on this broken people so strongly that the whole world will stand in awe of God, be drawn to God. "Nations shall come…" Isaiah gives the now dispirited people a vision of the coming glory in verse 4. All the scattered people of Judah will return. In verses 5 and 6 all the things the people now lack in their great poverty will come flowing to them from the farthest reaches of the world. The joy which the Lord will bring to his people will show forth God's goodness and mercy to the whole world.

In this text we also hear echoes of the Advent text "The people who walked in darkness have seen a great light; those who lived in a land of deep darkness--on them light has shined." (Isaiah 9:2). During the Church's season of Epiphany we celebrate God's gift of light that shows us who God really is. We celebrate the wonderful relief of finally being able to see clearly. We rejoice because the light makes it possible for us to act in this darkened world, to do the works of God.

Searching For the Light

The readings for all three cycles of the Lectionary are the same for Epiphany Day. One reason for this is that the story of the Wise Men is found only in Matthew's Gospel. **Read Matthew 2:1-2**.

Magi can mean foreign priests, magicians, and/or astrologers, or perhaps even emissaries of some kind. In AD 66 a delegation of Parthian magi paid homage to Nero at Naples (and returned home by another route). The New Testament and the rabbis writing in ancient days almost always saw magi as evil (see Acts 13:8-12). In the literature of the ancient Mediterranean area, stories about the birth of great men frequently contained signs in the stars and royal visitors.

However, it would be an especially sad mistake to see in Matthew's story only a tale about exotic mystery men and magical stars. The truth is that what is important in this text could be told without magi or heavenly portents. It is more important to hear what Matthew is proclaiming to us about the nature of Jesus Christ than to wonder over wise men and stars.

The Battle of the Kings

Read Matthew 2:3-12. Herod, who ruled from 40 BC to 4 BC was an Idumean half-Jew who ruled over Palestine as a puppet king for the Roman Empire. He had been an officer in the Roman army. His kingship was a reward from the Senate for his military service. Herod was a vicious brute of a man. **Read Matthew 2:13-18.**[1] The "Slaughter of the Innocents" as verses 16-18 are often called, would have been just his style. Herod had his own son murdered as well as other of his relatives. The magi made a serious tactical error in asking directions to a new "king" from the power-mad Herod!

Jesus is apparently two years old when the magi arrive and is living in Bethlehem ("On entering the house," 2.11). His family only moves to Nazareth to stay out of Archelaus' jurisdiction. Matthew and Luke (who tells us that Nazareth was Jesus' "home town") would not be concerned with the discrepancy over where Jesus lived. Remember, they are not interested in writing history as we understand history. They are writing theology; they are telling the truth about who Jesus is and about what his coming means. Just so, the movement of the "star" in verses 9 and 10 is not the way any real star moves. A star was sometimes thought of in the ancient world as a "fravashi," the counterpart or angel of a great man. The purpose of the star, as well as that of the magi themselves, is to highlight the fact that in Jesus we have an event that is of universal importance. Matthew may have added the detail of gold, frankincense, and myrrh to call to mind Isaiah 60. These are gifts fit for a king. Myrrh was also used as one of the "spices" in embalming. The fact that Matthew lists three gifts is the basis for the assumption that there were three magi.

The real point of Matthew's story is to show the reaction of worldly power to the announcement of the coming of God's power. The Gospel message is not "good news" to everyone. The "Herods" of the world rage against the coming of God's power into their spheres of influence. It is not that they ignore the Gospel, or are not convinced by the Gospel: they hate the Gospel with its message of the power of life and love over their powers of hate and death. In our day, Roman Catholic Archbishop Oscar Romero of El Salvador, gunned down while saying Mass, was a victim of those who hate the Gospel. Romero was a preacher of the Gospel of God to the poor. The rich did not want

---

1   Verses 13-18 are not part of the text for Epiphany Day, but they are part of the story that is one piece in Matthew's Gospel.

the peasants to have justice under God, for the peasants were their source of cheap labor. The powers of this world—hatred, greed, death—are terrified by the power of God and will always, in subtle or not-so-subtle ways, do all they can to destroy it.

In this Epiphany text the power of God, the will of God, the message of God, appears for the joy of all people on earth; but the powerful of the world, represented by Herod, never rejoice at this announcement. The Herods can slaughter little children, but they cannot destroy the power of God that has been made manifest in Jesus. Instead Herod dies (verse 19) and Jesus lives. If the Church is to convey the message of Epiphany, it had better not get tangled up in worrying about what star that might have been or what kind of people the magi were. The message that the Church has to proclaim is a crucial message for today. It is the message about the in-breaking of the power and love of God; a message of justice that always sets the Church against a world that only knows how to snatch and grab at the powers of destruction and death.

God's Plan Revealed

Read Ephesians 3:1-12. This text is an obvious choice for Epiphany since it announces the manifestation of the Gospel to the Gentiles, those who are not Jews. Jesus was the fulfillment of all the promises to Israel. All the very first Christians were Jews. Their nation was at the time in a life or death struggle with Gentiles, the Roman Empire. It therefore took the early Church some time to understand that the Gospel of Jesus Christ was also for non-Jews. It indeed came as revelation to Paul, to Peter, and to the whole Church that the good news of God's love and forgiveness was also for those beyond Judaism. The book of Acts (especially chapters 10, 11, and 15) deals with this watershed idea in the life of the Church.

Ephesians is a letter written to Gentile Christians. In verses 1-3 the readers are reminded that it was God and God alone who had "commissioned" Paul to take up missionary activity among the Gentiles. The "mystery" that was made known was the eternal purpose of God, which has always been, but has not always been revealed. In fact, its full revelation has come only in Jesus.

We Are One Body

In verse 6, the content of the eternal purpose of God is articulated: "that is, the Gentiles have become fellow heirs, members of the same body, and sharers in the promise in Christ Jesus through the Gospel." God's power is revealed as being a love great enough to embrace all nations ("ethne" in the Greek). God's purpose is for everyone to become one body in Christ. Racism and nationalism then are shown as antithetical to the purpose of God for humanity. For this reason, many liturgical churches have traditionally celebrated "race relations" Sundays during Epiphany. It is a happy coincidence that Martin Luther King, Jr.'s birthday falls during Epiphany. Paul rejoices that it is his glad duty to make known to the Gentiles "the boundless riches of Christ." Here, then, is also the Church's task at all times and in all places: to show to those outside the Church such love, compassion, mercy, and hope that the Church will reflect the very light of God. It is this light, not arguments or force, that will bring others to rejoice in God.

However, God's plan for the Church of Jesus Christ is even more ambitious! Verse 10 declares that the Church is to make known "the wisdom of God in its rich variety" to "the rulers and authorities in the heavenly places." Many people of the first century AD believed that the stars and planets (the wandering stars) each had a sentient being or "angel." These beings could be friendly or evil. They were not seen as agents of God. Christian teachers considered them evil. But they were no obstacle to the Gospel! The Church was to proclaim the truth revealed in Jesus Christ even to the "principalities and powers" in the heavenly places. By what Christians in the Church said and did out in the world, even the evil powers of the present age would come to see the revealed truth about the plan of God!

Those principalities and powers are not to be dismissed by moderns. Although we may not believe in evil or good beings attached to stars, we know that there are principalities and powers at work: hatred, destruction, cruelty, division, revenge, anger, prejudice, jealousy, gossip, and the like have power to destroy the human spirit. But, says verse 12, we have "access to God" that cannot be blocked by these powers. That access is faith in "Christ Jesus our Lord."

The mission of the Church is clearly set in the message of Epiphany. The Church exists to model in itself unity across all races and nations and types of people. The Church exists to reach out to the whole world by living out the message of the love and the glory of God that has been revealed to us in Jesus. It is to persevere in the face of all evil, all power, all threats, because the Church has access to God through faith in Jesus. The Church exists for the world. It exists to be a lamp shining in a dark place.

For Further Study and Reflection

Memory Bank

1. Memorize Isaiah 60:1-3.

Research

1. Find out more about Archbishop Oscar Romero. Check newspaper files or the Internet.

2. Read one of Martin Luther King, Jr.'s books such as **Where Do We Go From Here? Or Chaos or Community**.

3. Learn more about the reign of Herod the Great.

Reflection

1. Why is it often difficult for many of us to "allow" Jesus to belong to other cultures? Is the Epiphany message good news to you?

2. Our Christmas tradition of gift-giving comes from the gifts given to Jesus by the Magi. Is your gift-giving out of control—has it lost its meaning? How can we give true gifts to Jesus? Is giving to the poor a way of giving to Christ?

3. How well does your congregation engage the world through mission? How can you work through your local church to help the church's message reach out to others?

4. Read all of Matthew 2. Reflect on the power struggle going on in this story.